How to use this Guide to Vi

Welcome to Vienna. This publication is designed to
ennese sights. Regardless of whether you have just a
or plan a stay of several days, we recommend to begin your trail in the geographic (and spiritual) centre of Vienna, namely ...

St. Stephen's Cathedral

Following your visit to the Cathedral we invite you to embark on a stroll through downtown Vienna. The spot occupied today by the prestigious boulevard "The Ring" is actually the site of a mediaeval city wall. For the time being, let us stay within the precincts of "The Ring". The title of this chapter is ...

A Guided Walk through Mediaeval Vienna

This initial phase of your city centre tour ends at the Dominican Church. The second stage commences just a few minutes' walk away at the Urania Observatory and focuses on the Vienna Ring, where mansion houses began to be erected from 1860 onwards, replacing the ancient city wall.

Vienna's grand boulevard: "The Ring"

We have devoted a separate chapter to Vienna's Hofburg Palace owing to the complexity of the subject. Depending on the amount of time at your disposal you can fit the buildings, squares and monuments of the imperial era into one of the two proposed tours. The option is yours!

Imperial Vienna: The Hofburg Palace

Similar to the Hofburg Palace, Schönbrunn Palace likewise has a special chapter assigned to it. You should plan a whole day to explore this former imperial summer residence including a visit to Europe's finest zoo.

Schönbrunn Palace

The "Gürtel" or Belt is another ring road encompassing Vienna and covers a distance of three to six kilometres from St. Stephen's Cathedral. This chapter summarises the sights situated within the "Gürtel" or those close to the city centre that can be accesses to both quickly and easily by public transport.

Belvedere Palace, Prater Park, Hundertwasser & Co.

© Gerhard Vlcek

The top ten sights of Vienna

St. Stephen's Cathedral (page 11)
Vienna's landmark and one of the world's finest gothic churches

Schönbrunn Palace (page 58)
Masterpiece of baroque architecture and summer residence of the Habsburgers

Prater, Giant Ferris Wheel (page 68)
Gigantic amusement park and recreational area frequented by the local citizens

Hofburg Palaces (page 48)
An area steeped in imperial history, crowned by the New Hofburg Palace

Vienna State Opera (page 35)
Ranking among the world's leading opera houses

St. Charles' Church (page 33)
Created by the world renowned architect in his day, Fischer von Erlach

Vienna Civic Hall (page 44)
One of the many historic structures gracing "The Ring"

Imperial burial vaults (page 21)
Burial place in Vienna of the Habsburgs and Habsburg Line of Lorraine

Naschmarkt markets (page 34)
120 market-stall proprietors have been trading here for over a century

Danube Tower (page 70)
Austria's highest building (252 metres tall) commands fantastic views

Prominent personalities of Vienna ...

Dear Augustine *(*1643; †1685 in Vienna); The legendary singer chanted his ballads on the site of Vienna's Meat Market where he is honoured by a commemorative plaque (page 28).*

Johann Bernhard Fischer von Erlach *(*1656 in Graz; †1723 in Vienna), the baroque architect responsible for building many notable edifices.*

Maria Theresia *(*1717; †1780 in Vienna); managed the affairs of the state on behalf of her husband Emperor Francis Stephan of Lorraine; had Schönbrunn Palace built.*

Wolfgang Amadeus Mozart *(*1756 in Salzburg; †1791 in Vienna); spent ten years of his life in Vienna where he composed operas such as "The Magic Flute" (see page 20).*

Johann Strauss *(junior, *1825; †1899, in Vienna); the conductor and composer universally hailed as the "King of Waltz" achieved world fame with his "Blue Danube Waltz".*

Emperor Franz Joseph *(*1830; †1916 in Vienna); head of the Austro-Hungarian Monarchy for 68 years which collapsed shortly after his death.*

Elisabeth *("Sisi", *1837 in Munich; †1898 in Geneva); the daughter of a Bavarian duke, she married Franz Joseph in 1854 in the Church of St. Augustine/ Augustinerkirche in Vienna.*

Otto Wagner *(*1841; †1918 in Vienna); Austria's most celebrated architect at the turn of the 19th/20th century; achieved world fame for his Art Nouveau style edifices (see page 31).*

Gustav Klimt *(*1862; †1918 in Vienna); a leading Austrian painter and representative of the Viennese Art Nouveau style. Today, his paintings fetch prices of up to 90 million Euros.*

Arthur Schnitzler *(*1862; † 1931 in Vienna); Austrian dramatist, representative of Viennese Modernism. Famous for "The Dream Story" and "The Vast Domain".*

Friedensreich Hundertwasser *(*1928 in Vienna; †2000 New Zealand); The Austrian painter and designer hailed as "Vienna's Gaudí" ("Hundertwasser House", see page 72).*

DER DOMSCHATZ

St. Stephen's Cathedral (Stephansdom)

St. Stephen's Cathedral is Vienna's most recognizable landmark and Austria's finest Gothic edifice.

In 1147, a consecrated Romanesque church stood on the site of the present building, surrounded by a cemetery. The West Façade dates from the 13th century along with the two "Pagan" Towers and the Giant's Door/Riesentor.

Between 1304 and 1340, Dukes Albrecht I and Albrecht II erected the Gothic (Albertine) Choir; the South Tower (rising to just under 137m/449ft.) finally attained completion in 1433.

The smaller and uncompleted North Tower remains a mystery. About 1450 the architect Hans Puchsbaum was to have designed a tower exceeding the size and grandeur of the South Tower. Even today it is unclear as to whether work had to be suspended in 1515 due to financial reasons or whether by then the (Gothic) style was no longer in tune with the spirit of the times. The fact is that the tower reveals a height of only 68m/223 ft. It was not until 1578 that the Saphoy Brothers topped the Gothic torso with a conspicuous Renaissance cap.

Master sculptor Anton Pilgram was responsible for a number of interior features created between 1511 and 1516, as for example the cathedral pulpit and organ base. Nevertheless, following general conversion to the Baroque style in the 17th century, existing Gothic furnishings are fragmentary. None of the original 34 Gothic winged altars has been preserved. The Wiener Neustadt Altar of 1447 – one of the art-historical gems of the present-day interior furnishings – was only added to the Cathedral in 1883.

While the Cathedral remained unscathed during World War II, civilian plunderers set the building on fire in April 1945 causing serious damage. The timber framework of the roof was devastated by the flames and the great 22-ton cathedral bell, the "Pummerin", came crashing down out of its wooden bell cage. Reconstruction work commenced after the end of the war. In 1952 the Cathedral was reopened with a festive inauguration of the recast bell.

The altarpiece of 1474 of the "Schottenkirche", founded by Iro-Scottish monks, depicts the cathedral largely as we know it today.

Before you enter St. Stephen's we invite you to view the exterior of the Cathedral and – time permitting – to walk round the outside of the building. A climb of 343 steps takes you up to the spire of the imposing gothic south tower, effort rewarded by some really breath-taking views (open daily 9.30 am to 5 pm, admission € 4,–).

The main entrance: The two Pagan Towers and the Giant Gateway (13th century).

Exception to the rule: The smaller north tower with its conspicuous renaissance cap.

St. Stephen's Square appears somewhat small compared to the loftiness of the Cathedral.

The roof of the Cathedral is covered with some 230,000 tiles.

The entrance to (and exit from) St. Stephen's Cathedral Church is by the Giant Gateway. The Cathedral is open from 6 am to 10 pm (Sundays and public holidays from 7 am). No touring of the Cathedral is allowed during services. Otherwise there is a wide and varied range of guided tours which include the catacombs, the south tower and the cathedral treasury. An all-inclusive ticket can be had for € 16,–.

Master sculptor Anton Pilgram was responsible for a number of interior features created between 1511 and 1516, as for example the cathedral pulpit.

© Florian Monheim

© Florian Monheim

© Florian Monheim

Top left: Detail at the base of the Pilgram pulpit showing a window-gawking figure known as the Fenstergucker (fenster = window; gucker = person who gawks);

Top right: At the base of the organ a self-portrait of the sculptor Anton Pilgram, who crafted essential interior furnishings between 1511 and 1516;

To the left: Following general conversion to the Baroque style in the 17th century, existing Gothic furnishings are fragmentary. None of the original 34 Gothic winged altars has been preserved. The Wiener Neustadt Altar of 1447 – one of the art-historical gems of the present-day interior furnishings – was only added to the Cathedral in 1883.

The impressive Gothic vaulted ceiling of the triple-nave Cathedral

Another art-historical treasure piece is the Madonna of the Servants/Dienstbotenmadonna.

The high altar is an early Baroque masterpiece built to a design of the Pock Brothers.

The miraculous image of the Pócs Madonna has been in St. Stephen's Cathedral since 1697.

Vienna 1493: Clearly recognisable is the majestic Cathedral Church, the church "St. Mary on the Shore" (right) and the city gate to the northeast, the "Rotenturmtor".

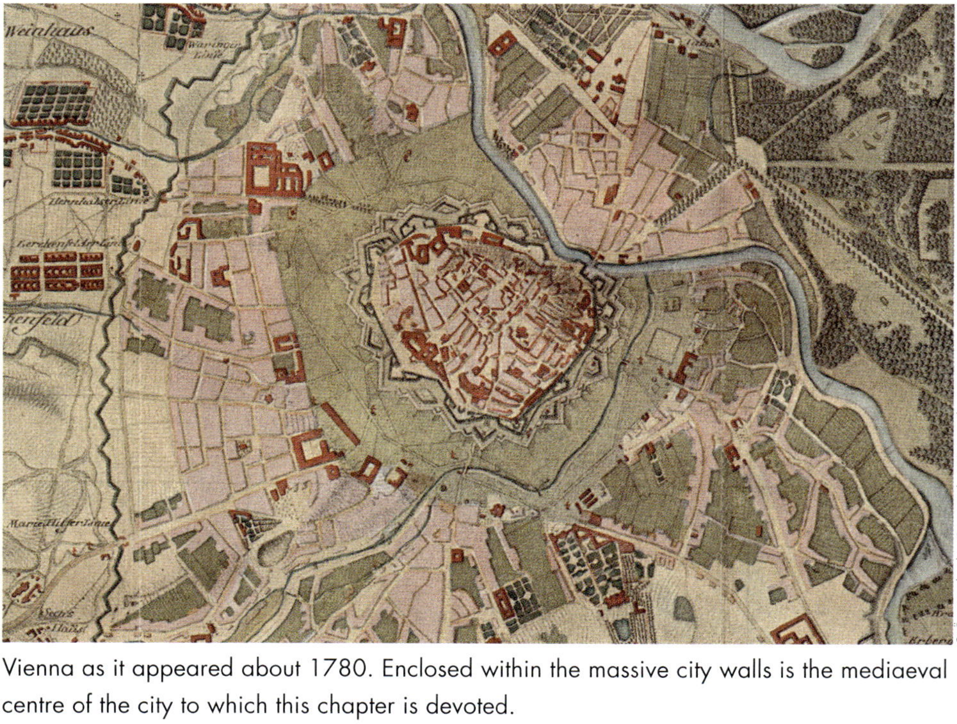

Vienna as it appeared about 1780. Enclosed within the massive city walls is the mediaeval centre of the city to which this chapter is devoted.

Walking tour of mediaeval Vienna

While ninth-century Vienna boasted a fortress, market ("Hoher Markt") and church (Ruprechtskirche), the city did not attain historical significance until after 1130 when the Babenberg dynasty acquired Merchants' Square. Vienna's rapid development was closely associated with Heinrich II (1107–1177), who in 1145 turned Vienna into the capital of what eventually became the Duchy of Ostarrichi (Austria). Heinrich erected a palace and domestic outbuilding on a site still known as "Am Hof" (royal court). In 1147 a small church was consecrated, then outside the town walls – the forerunner of today's St. Stephen's Cathedral. Heinrich II also founded the Iro-Scottish Monastery/ Schottenkloster in which he lies buried.

Alighting at the Metro Station "Stubentor" one encounters remains of the city wall erected by Duke Leopold V (1157–1194) and demolished in the 19th century. The two main gates leading into the city were the Carinthia Gate/Kärntnertor in the south and the Red Tower Gate/Rotenturmtor in the north. Initial mention of "Kärntnerstraße" goes back to 1257. This road eventually became known as "Venedigerstraße" owing to its further course continuing on right through to Venice.

Adriatic trading proceeded from "Neuer Market". The size of two football fields, this trading place provided adequate space for numerous buyers and sellers in addition to artisans.

In line with the rapid growth of the city, the Schottenkloster was soon joined by other monasteries, the Franciscan Friars being the first, followed by Dominican and Augustinian orders. By1500, some 750 monks were responsible for the pastoral care of Vienna's 20,000 inhabitants. As far back as 1237 mention is made of a school close to St. Stephen's. Opposite the cathedral church, a field dispensary "Zum goldenen Greif" was founded in 1320. This still operates today under the name "Alte Feldapotheke" (Old Field Dispensary).

Fires posed a serious threat, frequently devastating up to one third of the city. Erection of the city walls coincided with structural improvements involving the use of stone and tiled roofs, eventually followed by chimneys, fire walls and merlons.

There is mention of a hangman in the 13th century who later took up quarters in Rauhensteingasse Lane. This hangman's house ("Schergenhaus") also served as a jail and torture chamber.

Winding roadways were common in medieval times and served to impede enemy assault. About 1500, Emperor Ferdinand I introduced a type of tennis game to Vienna from Spain resulting in a number of ballgame houses or halls being erected. Certain street names are still a reminder of this.

On leaving St. Stephen's Cathedral through the Giant Gateway, glance to your left and you will notice the striking glass façade of the Haas House opened in 1990. This part of St. Stephen's Square is called the "Stock-im-Eisen-Platz". Two broad shopping malls branch out at this point: "Graben" and **Kärntner Street.**

Kärntner Straße already existed at the time of the Romans. In medieval times it linked the town centre with Carinthia Gate/Kärntnertor. Today it is a shopping boulevard similar to those normally found in larger European cities.

© Mozarthaus Vienna/David Peters

Short Detour, Part 1: Quaint winding lanes are to be found tucked away behind the Cathedral. Mozart once resided in Domgasse lane No. 5, commemorated by a museum.

Short Detour, Part 2: Branching off from Kärntner Street into Weihburggasse Lane ushers you into Franziskanerplatz, a picturesque square.

Before arriving at The Ring take a look to your right to admire the city's most famous hotel, the Sacher Hotel along with the Opera House (see page 35). If you now walk back a little towards St. Stephen's Cathedral and veer off at Johannesgasse Lane, this will bring you to what is referred to as the New Market/**Neuer Markt.**

© Van Bakel/picturedesk.com

The name is deceiving since "Neuer Markt" is in fact one of the oldest squares in Vienna, first mentioned in initial records dating back to 1234. The fountain was created by the celebrated sculptor Georg Raphael Donner from 1737 to 1739.
Pictured left is the Church of the Capuchin Friars on Neuer Markt completed in 1632. Despite its unimposing visual appearance it houses the imperial crypt.

The Imperial Crypt contains the remains of all German and Austrian emperors since 1633 except for one. The larger image above shows the tombs of Empress Elisabeth known as "Sisi" (1837–1898) (sarcophagus on left), Emperor Franz Joseph I (1830–1916, centre) and Crown Prince Rudolph (1858–1889, right).

Now walk across Neuer Markt and Seilergasse Lane in the direction of St. Stephen's Cathedral and you will automatically meet up with **"Graben"** (Ditch), another attractive strolling mall. At the end of the square, turn left to enter **Kohlmarkt.**

What today stands out as a grand boulevard and exclusive shopping mile was in Roman times in fact a ditch, filled in during the 12th century as Vienna underwent urban expansion. Interesting buildings include the baroque Bartolotti-Partenfeld mansion house (No. 11) and Ankerhof (Anchor Court) erected in 1894/95 by Otto Wagner (No. 10).

© lauqueur/picturedesk.com

Just a stone's throw away from Graben lies Dorotheergasse Lane where Leopold Hawelka (1911–2011) and his wife Josefine opened their legendary coffeehouse in 1939. Shortly up to his death Hawelka arrived daily to spend a few hours in his café.

Be sure not to overlook St. Peter's Church (Peterskirche). Consecrated in 1733, the interior abounds in baroque art treasures.

Graben's Trinity Column was erected in 1679 as a token of gratitude for success in overcoming a terrible plague epidemic.

Kohlmarkt is commonly known as Luxury Mile on account of the close network of jewellers and top-class brands found there. The street name has been in existence since the 14th century, the time when charcoal was sold on this spot.

270° panorama view (from left): Looshaus (built in 1909/10) ranks as one of the central edifices representing Viennese Modernism; Kohlmarkt; St. Michael's Church one of the few romanesque buildings in Vienna (erected about 1220); St. Michael's Gate (see page 53).

A stroll up and through Kohlmarkt will bring you to St. Michael's Square/ **Michaelerplatz.** We recommend you to visit Vienna's Hofburg Palace (see description on page 48) and resume your tour of the city in **Herrengasse.** Having reached the end of Herrengasse you will encounter yet another of Vienna's fine squares, the **Freyung.**

Ferstel House in Herrengasse, formerly the headquarters of the Stock Exchange, is where today the Café Central welcomes its guests.

A short detour to the Minorites Church is worthwhile. This is one of the most beautiful gothic edifices in Vienna.

With its magnificent city palais, Freyung Square is one of the finest in Vienna's Old Town. The Iro-Scottish Monastery founded in 1155 has continued to dominate the square down to the present day. Freyung Square is chiefly known for its markets, in particular the Easter Market or the Old Vienna Christmas Fair.

Now proceed down Freyung in the direction of St. Stephen's Cathedral. After walking a few steps you will set foot on a square called **"Platz am Hof".** Cross the square and you will find yourself on **Judenplatz** or Jews Square.

"Am Hof" Square lays claim to historic significance: it was here – in the heart of medieval Vienna – that the Babenbergs resided (predecessors of the Habsburgs) from 1155 up to about 1280. The church is essentially Gothic but was given an impressive baroque façade in 1607 following an outbreak of fire.

Platz am Hof: The magnificent baroque façade adorning the former arsenal.

On Judenplatz – mediaeval Centre of the Jewish Community in Vienna – a memorial is erected for the 65,000 Austrian Jews murdered during the Second World War.

We now leave the Jewish Quarter via Fütterergasse Lane. Crossing Wipplinger St. brings you to the Church of St. Mary on the Shore **(Maria am Gestade).** Then retrace your steps to Wipplingergasse leading to **Hoher Markt Square.**

The Bohemian Court Chancellery built from 1709 to 1714 by Fischer von Erlach now houses the Constitutional Court.

Maria am Gestade is one of Vienna's oldest churches; the characteristic Gothic spire underwent completion in 1428.

Hoher Markt – the principal market during the Middle Ages – is Vienna's oldest square. The Marriage Fountain was erected in 1792.

The Ankeruhr Clock on Hohen Markt Square. This horologic masterpiece designed in art nouveau style was erected in 1914.

Leaving Hoher Markt, turn into **Judengasse** Lane. Located couple of steps away is **St. Ruprecht's Church.** Continuing via Fleischmarkt (Meat Market) and Postgasse your path will take you to the **Jesuit Church,** ending at the **Dominican Church.**

First recorded in 1200, Ruprechtskirche (above) is Vienna's oldest surviving church. It is dedicated to St. Rupert, the patron saint of salt merchants and founder of the City of Salzburg. The narrow lanes built around Ruprechtskirche are known as the Bermuda Triangle/Bermudadreieck.

The Meat Market is where Greek merchants settled about 1700. Their trysting place was the "Greek Inn" situated in Griechengasse.

According to legend, the ballad singer "Dear Augustin" frequented the area surrounding Griechenbeisl in the 1680s.

The Jesuit Church (bottom right), an early baroque edifice, owes its present-day appearance to the architect Andrea Pozzo.

The baroque Dominican Church (top right) took more than 40 years to build, finally undergoing completion in 1674. This is the second largest church in Vienna.

Sightseeing tour to discover some of the attractions in The Ring

By the mid 19th century at the latest, the city wall had ceased to have any further military significance and the fortifications were found to be hampering what were rapidly progressing urban development plans. While the citizens of Vienna had meanwhile come to appreciate the park-like glacis with its refreshment pavilions for its recreational facilities, Emperor Franz Joseph I made a bold decision on December 20, 1857 for the city wall to be razed to the ground and a boulevard to be erected in its place.

The "Ring" is more or less circular in shape and is well over 5 km (3 miles) in length, subdivided into nine sections from "Stubenring" to "Schottenring". Only Franz-Josefs-Kai situated north-east deviates from the strict geometrical pattern of the route.

Our tour begins and ends at the Danube Canal from where we will be making our way along The Ring in clockwise direction. Accordingly, our starting point is the **Urania,** a cinema and observatory once devoted to technical advancement.

Our tour begins and ends at the Danube Canal from where we will be making our way along The Ring in clockwise direction. Accordingly, our starting point is the Urania, a cinema and observatory once devoted to technical advancement.

The Postal Savings Bank building, hailed as a milestone of Viennese architecture at the turn of the 19th/20th century, is considered to be Otto Wagners major work.

The first museum to be built in the "Ring" was designed by Heinrich von Ferstel, its present day funktion is that of a Museum of Applied Art, better known as MAK.

One of the most frequently photographed monuments of Vienna is the gilt bronze statue of Johann Strauss II (top) erected in the Vienna City Park/Stadtpark. Designed by Edmund Hellmer, it was unveiled on June 26, 1921.

At **Schwarzenbergplatz** Square (look at those splendid mansion houses!) we leave The Ring and proceed down Lastenstraße Street running parallel to The Ring, making a detour leading us to **Naschmarkt** or Victuals Market.

Inaugurated in 1899, Karlsplatz Station, forming part of Vienna's former Metropolitan Railway, numbered among the best known Art Nouveau structures in the city. Conversion to underground train operations from 1976 to 1981 resulted in the station undergoing radical change. However, the two richly ornamented pavilions erected by Otto Wagner remained preserved.

This well testifies to the supply of high-quality spring water on Schwarzenberg-platz Square since 1873.

Inaugurated in 1870, Vienna's Musik-verein is of major significance to music lovers throughout the world.

The Golden is a popular venue for the annual New Year's Day concert given by the Vienna Philharmonic Orchestra.

© www.foto-julius.at

St. Charles's Church/Karlskirche ranks among the most illustrious baroque places of worship north of the Alps. It owes its Italian character to Johann Bernhard Fischer von Erlach, a star architect of the period, who had undergone training in Rome. The façade symbolizes a Roman temple portico; the adjacent columns are modelled on Trajan's Column in Rome; the spiral staircases have their origins in the Eternal City.

Naschmarkt is a Viennese speciality. The atmosphere of this victuals market imparts a touch of zest to life in the city. The market was transferred to this spot from Freyung about 1780. Todays typical market stalls evolved around the year 1910. From Monday to Saturday fruits, vegetables, breads, pastries as well as fish and meat products are traded here, meanwhile enhanced by a good selection of restaurants.

In 1897 a group of artists belonging to the circle surrounding Gustav Klimt seceded from the conservative-minded Artists' Union and founded the Vienna Secession Association. This marked the birth of the Viennese Art Nouveau Style or Secessionist Style. One year after founding of the movement the Secessionist Exhibition Hall was built based on designs of Joseph Maria Olbrich who had studied with Otto Wagner.

If you have kept to route we have suggested, you will have meanwhile distanced yourself quite a way from The Ring. Return now to The Ring via Operngasse Lane where you will find yourself outside the Opera House (photo on pages 36/37).

© Jantzen/picturedesk.com

When in 1857 it was resolved to construct a stately boulevard, the first monumental structure planned to be built was the Imperial Court Opera House – now the Vienna State Opera. Neo-Renaissance in style, the edifice was designed by the Viennese architects Sicard von Sicardsburg and Van der Nüll and inaugurated on May 25, 1869 with a first-night performance of Mozart's "Don Giovanni".

© Schafler/picturedesk.com

The grand staircase. Large photo on pages 36/37: The State Opera viewed from the "Ring".

© Tuma/picturedesk.com

The Vienna Opera Ball/Wiener Opernball is Austria's leading high-society event. Its roots go back to the year 1877.

Sightseeing tour to discover some of the attractions in The Ring

Continuing around The Ring in clockwise direction you will see Hofburg Palace on your right which, on account of its complexity, is described in a separate chapter (see page 48). At this point we head for the museum district.

© www.foto-julius.at

The two buildings – the Museum of Art History and Museum of Natural History – are both arranged in symmetrical order. They form part of the Imperial Forum, an architectural project conceived by Gottfried Semper which was to have been the crowning glory of The Ring but failed to achieve completion. The monument between the two museums depicts Maria Theresa. The Museum of Art History evolved from collections acquired by the Habsburgers and is considered one of the most important of its kind in the whole world.

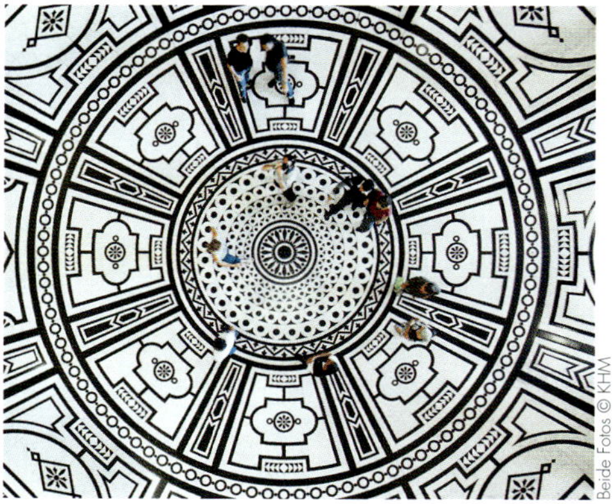

Beide Fotos © KHM

The Museum of Art History was inaugurated in 1891 and attracts over a million visitors each year. Illustrated here is the staircase and vestibule.

Important exhibits from the Museum of Art History:

Rembrandt (1606–1669): "Large Self-portrait"

Peter Paul Rubens (1577–1640): "The Fur" (section)

Albrecht Dürer (1471–1528): "Emperor Maximilian I"

Pieter Bruegel The Elder (c. 1525–1569): "Peasant Wedding" (section)

In the mood for a shopping spree? Mariahilfer Street, Vienna's main shopping mall, starts at the Museum Quarter. This boulevard has been closed to motor traffic since 2013 but beware of Viennese cyclists who tend to speed through the mall!

© Hochmuth/picturedesk.com

The Museum Quarter/Museumsquartier, opened in 2001, has proved a brilliant success. The former Imperial Stables (erected in 1725 by Fischer von Erlach) are devoted to contemporary art. In addition to a variety of restaurants, two important museums are situated at the Museum Quarter:

On display in the Leopold Museum is the Leopold Collection (Egon Schiele/Gustav Klimt) while …

… the Museum of Modern Art (MUMOK) contains works representing Classic Modern Art (Warhol, Picasso, Beuys, Johns).

The Austrian Houses of Parliament is where the legislative body of the Republic, the National Council, convenes. The building was designed by Theophil von Hansen in the Greco-Roman style and inaugurated in December 1883. Towering above the fountain is a 4m/13ft. high statue of Pallas Athene.

Located behind the Houses of Parliament is Vienna's Palace of Justice. It was built from 1875 to 1881 by Alexander Wielemans von Monteforte in Neo Renaissance style. Enjoy the fantastic view from the roof-top terrace of the Cafeteria (open to the public).

© www.foto-julius.at

Opposite – on The Ring – you will see the Vienna Civic Hall (top) and the Burgtheater (bottom right) separated by Rathausplatz Square.

© Sato/picturedesk.com

© Deak/picturedesk.com

Once destined for political rallies, the square outside the City Hall (Rathausplatz) is nowadays used for all types of events, e.g. ice-skating (left) or the Life Ball (right).

© Kurt Pultar

© Gerhard Vlcek

Vienna underwent substantial growth in 1850 when several suburbs were incorporated in the boundaries of the City. Accordingly, it was decided to build a larger City Hall along the "Ring". The façade is an outstanding example of Neo-Gothic civil architecture. The building measures 152m/498.7ft. in length and 127m/416.7ft. in width, and contains 1,575 rooms.

The Imperial Court Theatre/Burgtheater is classed among the leading German-language theatres. Up to 1888 it was located on Michaelerplatz square close to Hofburg Palace before removal to the Neo-Baroque edifice along the "Ring". The building was gutted after being hit by a bomb in 1945 and was not re-opened until ten years later. Design of the ceiling frescoes enhancing the two staircases included work by Gustav Klimt.

The main building of the University was erected between 1877 and 1884 by Heinrich von Ferstel.

The (old) Stock Exchange, erected from 1874 to 1877 in neo renaissance style, was also designed by Theophil von Hansen.

Votive Church was erected as a token of humble gratitude paid by Emperor Franz Joseph I after surviving an assassination. The towers rise to a height of 99m/324.5ft.

After suffering serious damage in World War II, inauguration of the 73m/239.5ft. high-rise Ring Tower in 1955 proved a milestone in the reconstruction of the City.

Imperial Vienna – Hofburg Court Palace

Although no exact date is traceable, the Bohemian King Ottokar II Premysl, began building a fortress and moat in the mid 13th century or thereabouts exactly on the site where today the Swiss Wing of the Hofburg is located. By the time this edifice received first official mention in 1279 (then not a palace but merely a fortification complex with a keep) Ottokar had already been defeated. He was followed by the first Roman-German king from the House of Habsburg, Rudolf I.

The Hofburg is anything but a uniform structure. In fact it developed over a period of six centuries. Extensions continued on this irregular set of buildings from the time of Ferdinand I, who reigned from 1531 to 1564 and who was the first of the Habsburgs to feel at home in Vienna, through to Franz Joseph I (1848–1916, top) who set the course for Vienna becoming a metropolis. Development took place without respect for architectural perspective. Accordingly, the huge complex resembles an incidental hotchpotch of widely differing styles.

We recommend you to begin your tour of the Vienna Hofburg Palace on Michaelerplatz Square. However, instead of passing directly through Michaelertor Gate (see photo below) proceed left, past the gateway and enter Reitschulgasse Lane.

On your left in Reitschulgasse Lane you will see the Royal Stables of the Spanish Riding School. The school was originally used by members of the imperial family for equestrian training purposes and is now listed as a UNESCO world heritage site. Situated on your right is the entrance to the Winter Riding School inaugurated in 1735 (bottom photo). The Lipizzan stallions (pictured right) are the world's oldest pure-bred horses.

Reitschulgasse Lane opens out on to Josefsplatz Square. Pictured on the left is the entrance to the National Library with the wing housing the Grand Redoubt Ballroom on the right. The mounted statue is that of Emperor Josef II. Also located on Josefsplatz is the entrance to …

… the church of St. Augustine. Consecrated in 1349, this gothic place of worship initially stood alone on the site, the surrounding buildings not emerging until later. In 1634 St. Augustine's became the Imperial Court Chapel where marriage ceremonies of the Habsburgers took place.

The Royal Library (today the Austrian National Library) was designed according to the plans of Johann Bernhard Fischer von Erlach and underwent completion in 1735. The Baroque Great Hall ranks among the world's most impressive library rooms.

Passing through Augustiner St. brings you to yet another edifice forming part of the Hofburg Palace complex, Archduke Albrecht House, which maintains a superb graphic art collection with exhibits from the late gothic era down to the present day – the far-famed Albertina.

© Thomas/picturedesk.com

To access to the castle gardens simply proceed around the Albertina. The conservatory (Palmenhaus) contains a tropical butterfly house as well as a popular restaurant and café.

Having introduced you to the east-side of Hofburg Palace, let us now venture into the heart of the former Imperial Court of Vienna. To do this, we will need to retrace our steps back to our starting point, St. Michael's Gate (see page 48).

Joseph Emanuel Fischer von Erlach had already planned St. Michael's Wing back in 1726. Nevertheless, it took well over 150 years to complete this impressive edifice with its awe-inspiring dome after the old Imperial Court Theatre/ Burgtheater had been removed to Ringstraße.

© picturedesk.com

Passing through St. Michael's Gate brings you to the inner courtyard. Amelienburg is one of the oldest constructions making up Hofburg Palace and was erected to serve as residence for Emperor Rudolph II (1552–1612). Originally a freestanding structure, it is today adjoined to the Leopoldine Wing (pictured left) and the Imperial Chancellery (right).

The red-black Swiss Gate/Schweizertor on which the titles of Emperor Ferdinand I are displayed along with the insignia of the Order of the Golden Fleece forms the entrance to the Swiss Court (Schweizer Hof). This corresponds in its form to the 13th century castle except that it was converted to the Renaissance style during the mid 16th century.

Fotos in der linken Spalte © KHM

The Swiss Court contains the Gothic Court Chapel rebuilt in the 15th century and the Imperial Treasury/Schatzkammer.

Viewed on left, top to bottom: Austrian imperial crown; cradle of Napoleon's son, a gift of the City of Paris to Napoleon Bonaparte and Marie Louise; emerald unguentarium of 1641, one of the world's largest emeralds.

Continuing further through a second gate you get to Heldenplatz (Heroes) square and the New Imperial Palace (Neue Hofburg). This is the most recent addition to the Imperial

Quarter. Architecturally speaking it represents Historicism, a style shared by other buildings along The Ring that went up in 1860 or thereabouts.

Schönbrunn is about 5 kilometres distance from the centre of Vienna and can be reached by Underground (Line U4). The Palace is open daily 8.30 am to 5 and 6.30 pm (depending on the time of year). Guided tours are available from € 11.50.

Schönbrunn Palace and Zoo

Vienna owes its important monuments, such as Karlskirche or the Great Hall of the National Library, to the celebrated Baroque architect Johann Bernhard Fischer von Erlach (1656–1723). Schönbrunn Palace is also based on his plans even if Maria Theresia, who loved the place, set about having it converted to a residential palace designed by Nikolaus Pacassi as from 1744.

The historical significance of Schönbrunn is immense: for centuries it was the summer residence of the Habsburgs. Napoleon took up quarters here between 1806 and 1809 as well as the European rulers during the Vienna Congress of 1814/15. Emperor Franz Joseph I was born and died in Schönbrunn. In 1918, Emperor Karl I signed the document renouncing all participation in state affairs, thus sealing the end of the Danube Monarchy.

Following expropriation of the Imperial Court, ownership of the palace passed to the Republic of Austria. It became recognized by UNESCO as a world heritage site in 1996 and attracts approximately two million visitors a year.

In the 1780s Emperor Joseph II commissioned all noble edifices within the Austro-Hungarian State to be painted in "Schönbrunn Amber".

© Wiesenhofer/Österreich Werbung

Schönbrunn Palace, north façade with forecourt.

View of the gardens from the Gloriette and the south façade of Schönbrunn Palace.

© www.foto-julius.at

Approximately 40m/130ft. in length, the Grand Gallery (top left) forms the heart of the palace. The ceiling frescoes are the work of the Italian artist Gregorio Guglielmi. Other state apartments: Rösselzimmer, literally Stallions Room (top right); Marie Antoinette Salon (centre left); Chinese Salon (centre right) used by Maria Theresia for privy conferences; Vieux Laque Salon (bottom right) Emperor Franz (I) Stephan's study.

© Gerhard Vlcek

Erected in 1775, the Gloriette provides a spectacular view of the gardens covering 1.6 sq.m/17.2 sq.ft.

© Schafler/picturedesk.com

In 1880 Emperor Franz Joseph I commissioned the Palm House to be built in order to create a worthy setting for the Habsburg collection of tropical plants.

In 1736 the Habsburg-Lorraine dynasty was formed as a result of the marriage of the Duke of Lorraine, later to become Emperor Franz (I) Stephan of Lorraine, with Archduchess and Habsburg heiress Maria Theresia (pictured above).
It was a happy marriage from which 16 children proceeded. Though never crowned empress, Maria Theresia managed the affairs of the monarchy for 40 years. She implemented essential reforms and set numerous monuments in memory of herself.

Schönbrunn Zoo is one of the finest in Europe. There are no fewer than 730 species to admire spread over 17 hectares of space. The zoo is open daily from 9 am and closes at 4.30 pm in winter and 6.30 pm in summer. Admission € 16.50.

Emperor Franz (I) Stephan of Lorraine, who left it to his wife Maria Theresia to manage the state affairs, devoted himself to natural sciences. In 1752 he founded Schönbrunn Zoological Park (central photos) and one year later the Botanical Gardens. The zoo is the oldest in the world. It catered for a sensation in 2007 with the birth of panda baby Fu Long. Successful breeding of elephants and Siberian tigers also takes place here. The latest addition to the zoo is the "Franz Josef Land" Polar Bear Kingdom.

Embark on the ten-minute trek from The Ring to Schwarzenbergplatz Square to Belvedere Palace (or simply board Tramline D). The entrance fees are rather steep, approx. € 12.50 for admission to the Upper Belvedere (open daily from 10 am to 6 pm), combined tickets up to € 30,–.

Belvedere Palace

After final victory over the Turks in 1683 and the annexation of Hungary, Vienna entered a glorious era. A spectacular witness of this period is the summer residence of the great military leader Prince Eugène of Savoy – Belvedere Palace. The baroque complex comprises the stately palace "Upper Belvedere" constructed from 1721 to 1723. The conspicuously smaller garden palace "Lower Belvedere" had already undergone completion in 1716. The two are linked by attractive gardens.

Both these palaces were designed by Johann Lucas von Hildebrandt (1668–1745), whose fame as an architect is comparable to that of Johann Bernhard Fischer von Erlach. After Prince Eugène's death, Belvedere came under the ownership of the Habsburgs. Today it houses an art collection of significance – the Belvedere Austrian Gallery.

Lower Belvedere had already undergone completion in 1716.

In the Golden Room stands a marble statue crafted about 1718 by Balthasar Permoser.

The Main Gate supports the armorial bearings of Prince Eugène, the lion.

© Trumler/Imagno/picturedesk.com

From the very outset, Upper Belvedere was planned for prestige purposes, the lower palace mainly being used as a residence.
Picture to the left: The Sala Terrena on the ground floor is an Italian-style garden hall, whose design may be ascribed to the years of study in Rome by the architect, Johann Lukas von Hildebrandt.
The Belvedere art collection is one of the most significant in the world. Below (left to right) paintings by Gustav Klimt ("The Kiss"), Ferdinand Georg Waldmüller and Claude Monet.

The gateway to the Prater Amusement Park is just three underground stations (Line U1) away from St. Stephen's Cathedral ("Praterstern" Station). The U2 also stops here. If it's the park and recreation you are seeking, it might be better to board Tramline 1.

The Prater Park

In most cases, the Wiener Prater is associated solely with the world-famous amusement park. It is frequently overlooked that this is a spacious public park, large parts of which still consist of river meadowland. The area of the Prater extends to 6 sq.km/2.3 square miles, three times larger than the Principality of Monaco. In 1564 Emperor Maximillian succeeded in purchasing the Prater from several landowners to create hunting grounds which he fenced off (hunting took place in the Prater up to 1920).

The Happel-Stadium was erected in 1931. With a capacity of 50,000 spectators it ranks among Europe's most prestigious football arenas.

In 1766, Emperor Joseph II released the Prater for public use and in so doing laid the foundation stone for launching the amusement park Wurstelprater as it eventually became known as.

© Jahn/picturedesk.com

The Giant Ferris Wheel/Riesenrad was inaugurated in 1897 to mark the golden jubilee of Emperor Franz Joseph I's accession to the throne. At that time it was the largest giant wheel in the world.

The Danube divides Vienna's metropolitan area. The city centre lies west of the river and the business area Danube City with its notable skyscrapers on the east bank. Danube Island is a popular recreation spot frequented by the locals (Underground Line U1).

Pictured right: The Danube Tower was officially opened in 1964 for the occasion of the Vienna Horticultural Show. With a height rising to 252 metres it ranks as Austria's tallest building. Those who find the descent by lift too unspectacular can opt for the bungee rope.

In 1972 heavy criticism was hurled at plans to land-fill Danube Island/Donauinsel (pictured above, viewed from Leopoldsberg) as part of an extensive project designed to counteract flooding. Today the Island, 21km/13 miles long and up to roughly 250m/820ft. broad, fulfils its purpose ideally and is regarded as indispensable by Viennese citizens as a recreational area. To landscape Danube Island, some 420 acres of woodland were planted.

© Chromorange/picturedesk.com

Danube City is a new urban area on the left bank of the Danube, whose development coincided with the inauguration of the United Nations Headquarters (UNO-City) in 1979.

The DC Tower (built to the plans of architect Dominique Perrault) was inaugurated in February 2014). It rises to a height of 220 metres.

Tramline 1 whisks you from The Ring to the Hundertwasser Krawina House in a matter of minutes (Station "Hetzgasse").

Hundertwasser-Krawina-Haus: Entwurf: Prof. J. Krawina; Maler: F. Hundertwasser; Planung: Prof. J. Krawina, P. Pelikan. Foto © Kurt Pultar

© Gerhard Vlcek

The artist Friedensreich Hundertwasser (1928–2000) designed a dwelling house erected in Vienna's Third District between 1983 and 1985 (Hundertwasser Krawina House, above). Hundertwasser was strongly influenced by the architecture of Antoni Gaudí.

A little remote from downtown Vienna is the Spittelau Waste Incinerator (pictured left), featuring another interesting example of Hundertwasser's art.